This book is for Zora.

I am so lucky I get to love you and now your sister too.

2024 My Canadian Family Paperback Edition

Copyright © 2024 Laura Lee Fedoryshin Prashad. Illustrations copyright © 2024 Laura Lee Fedoryshin Prashad. Initial illustrations for character design were contributed by Kenneth Togonon. All rights reserved. No part of this book may be reproduced or transmitted in any form or by any means, electronic or mechanical, including photocopying, recording, or by any information storage and retrieval system, without written permission from the author. For information address Laura@mycanadianfamily.ca

Printed in Canada
ISBN Softcover 978-1-0688862-0-1
ISBN Hardcover 978-1-0688862-1-8
ISBN Ebook 978-1-0688862-2-5

THIS BOOK BELONGS TO

Ok, my sweet girl, the baby is coming. Your sister is ready to leave Mommy's tummy. Soon, your life will be fuller than ever before because there will be more to love.

It's time to stay with Grampa and Gramms; I know you can do it; it's part of the plan. And soon we'll all be together, just like before. But there will be one more to love.

Come quietly now, whisper hello. You can touch her soft hands and kiss her little toe. And just like that, our family is bigger than ever before, and now we have more to love.

Loved ones will come to see the baby and big sister, too. They are always excited to watch the new things you can do. And the celebrations will be grander than ever before because now we have more to love.

It's exciting to welcome someone new. So we will take lots of pictures and smile while we do. And the pictures will be more stunning than ever before because now there's more to love

Sometimes, babies will cry, and the reason is unclear. We can comfort her with soft words and gentle pats that show her we're here. We will learn to be more compassionate than ever before because now there's more to love.

Babies can sometimes take a long time to eat; you can play quietly by yourself or sit with mom in her seat. We will need to be more patient than ever before because now there's more to love.

We will go out for walks and see the world through new eyes; we can stretch in the shade and get exercise. And the world will be brighter than ever before because now there's more to love.

We'll jump in muddy puddles and make lots of mess, so we'll take a bath and you'll need to undress. And the bath will be bubblier than ever before because now there's more to love.

You can make funny faces and say peekaboo, be silly and imagine like only siblings can do. And playtime will be more fun than ever before because now there's more to love.

The world has so much for you to discover. I'm so glad that now you can count on each other. Together, you can achieve more than ever before because now you have more to love.

You're so big now, you can do lots of things, like color with markers and go by yourself on the swings. But babies are easily hurt by sharp or small toys, so we need to be tidier than ever before, because now we have more to love.

We'll go on adventures and buckle up in the car; sometimes, our trips will be short, and sometimes, they'll be far. We'll see that the world is more enchanting than ever before because now we have more to love.

We'll play music loud and sing till we're blue, then dance round in circles cause it's fun to do. Together, we'll rock harder than ever before because now we have more to love.

If you feel frustrated, like things are changing too fast, we'll take deep breaths together until the tough moments have passed. Together, we'll breathe slowly and learn to be calmer than ever before because now we have more to love.

At the end of the day, we will say good night and cuddle as the sky fills with stars. As we drift off and dream, we will think of how lucky we are because now we have more to love.

A word from the Author

Your voice truly matters so if you enjoyed this book it would mean the world to me if you would take a short minute to leave a heartfelt review on Amazon. Your kind feedback is very appreciated and so very important. Thank you so much for your time.